when you ask WHY

It's OK to ask.

daniel e. johnson

New Leaf Press

First printing: February 2002
Third printing: December 2014

ISBN: 978-0-89221-712-0
Library of Congress Number: 2001098909

Unless otherwise noted, all Scripture references
are from the New King James Version of the
Bible.

Please consider requesting that a copy of this
volume be purchased by your local library
system.

Printed in the United States of America

Please visit our website for other great titles:
www.newleafpress.net

For information regarding author interviews,
contact the publicity department at (870) 438-5288.

To
David

We thought you left too soon.

Contents

FOREWORD

When You Ask Why is a classic. First written more than 20 years ago, now in its eighth printing, it speaks to all of us. It is worth reading, not because it answers the tough questions, but because it refuses to dismiss them — or to offer easy answers. Rereading the book evoked vivid memories of the many times I have sought for answers to life's dilemmas.

Daniel Johnson reminds us that our plans may sometimes be interrupted by a variety of circumstances. And we are not alone, he suggests. Joseph comes to mind. What grandiose dreams marked his youth! But the very dreams seemed to mock him when his brothers betrayed him and sold him into slavery. The long years in an

Egyptian prison were not what he had in mind when his youthful imagination had run wild. But the all-knowing God was never absent from Joseph's life, and in His own time, what was intended for evil became a blessing to his family and to the whole nation.

And why do we love the Psalms? Is it not, in part, because the shepherd boy who became a king and wrote so many of the Psalms, describes in poetic detail what it was like hiding from King Saul, fleeing from his own son, or pouring out his anguished heart to a God who seemed far away?

The Apostle Paul was certain that the hardships he faced were the stuff of which life is made, and that those things work for us "a far more exceeding and eternal weight of glory" (2 Corinthians 4:17). Paul had discovered a profound truth: *The secret of growing in grace is to be in a place where you need grace.* The secret of leaning hard on God is to be found in those circumstances in which you have no other choice.

The author of this volume writes that the experiences from which we shrink often prove to be the portals through which we advance to the richest and sweetest experiences of our lives. Given that trials may become a benediction in disguise, valleys may be more important than the mountains. Someone has observed that few of us can drink out of a full cup. There is far greater danger in conquest and victory than in loss and defeat. The Lord won't let us forget that. Our God is the God of the mountains, but He is God of the valleys as well, and He is faithful. This is the message of *When You Ask Why,* written out of a heart of compassion by Daniel Johnson. You will understand yourself better and love the Lord more deeply in reading this masterpiece.

Richard W. Dortch
Author, conference speaker, TV host

INTRODUCTION

This book was written two decades ago. It has been reissued a number of times, undergone two or three revisions and cover makeovers, and now carefully edited again with minor additions made. Because it touches on events occurring over a period of time and in different locations, an explanation is in order.

The careful reader will question the sequence of events and wonder about the time-line. No effort has been made to clarify times and places, to put them in proper order. We're living in Milwaukee on one page, in Charlotte on another, then moving across the country to Seattle on yet another. From disappointment in career to the collapse of the Twin Towers, the narrative stretches unevenly across the years.

You will say this doesn't make sense, this is no way to write a book. You may be right. But that's not the point. This is not a historical document or theological discussion. It is not an exercise in logic or argument. It is not likely to win a Pulitzer nor gain approval of the English teacher. The heart knows its own bitterness and there are feelings deeper than words. This is an invitation to track with a fellow struggler, to journey with a friend toward the Celestial City. By God's grace, and your generous help in looking after one another, we shall all travel safely to the river's edge.

I visited an old friend who was dying of lung cancer. I noticed two books — just two — on his nightstand: the Bible and a thin volume titled *Heaven* by E.M. Bounds. You travel light on the long journey my friend would take three or four days later. Speaking of eternal life, don't miss *On Resurrection* by my brother, Clayton Lee Johnson. Of the five boys and one girl in our family, it was agreed that he has the best brain.

I found a word the other day: *extrude.* Kind of an interesting word. It means "to thrust out; force or press out; expel: *to extrude molten rock.*" You get the picture of something good being forced out as a result of pressure, or pain, even. My brother's life has not been easy. Some of the words that have poured from his pen — extruded, if you will, have come at some cost, and will not soon be forgotten by those who have read them. Don't miss *On Resurrection.*

I am grateful to my daughter Cindy for carefully proofreading this manuscript. To my wife Martha, without whose editorial help and loving support these pages would be blank, saying thanks seems inadequate. Now, it's time to get started. What do you do, where do you go, when life tumbles in? Let's make the journey together.

On Resurrection

In my unwilling immolation
Spectral figures loom.
Unwelcome immigration
To my soul's burning room.
Again my heart remembers —
Where once was heady adulation
Is now a tomb.

How soon spring became September!
For one day my maturation
Vaulted to the stars.
Then spider-like came denigration,
Weaving webs like prison bars.

But with fire in every member
I hear a syncopation
Cascade from above:
No one lives in isolation,
There's a branch for every dove!

Now, reduced to one small ember,
My heart hears an indication
As by thunder from above:
Death is but initiation!
Afterword, comes breathless love!
So perish every accusation,
Every lying taunt that hell's of;
I shall rise to higher station
For securely in my heart is: Love!

Clayton Lee Johnson

The unexplained things
in life are more than the
explained. God seems careless as
to whether men understand him
or not; he scarcely vindicates
his saints to men.

(Oswald Chambers, 1874–1917)

CHAPTER ONE
WHEN LIFE
TUMBLES IN

The scenes are etched so deep in memory the soul seems scarred forever — planes plunging into towers, 110 floors collapsing on top of one another, thousands fleeing burning buildings and falling debris, and mountains of smoke and ash rising where Manhattan's magnificent towers once stood.

"Images of dazed New Yorkers swimming in ash will haunt our cultural memory," Jerry Adler wrote in *Newsweek*.[1]

It was a picture perfect day on the East Coast. September 11, 2001. We were well into the first year of the new century, and things looked promising all across the country. The economy was a little weak, but it would improve. It was a good time to review the past, count our blessings, and get a grip on the tasks that lay ahead.

That's what they were doing at Hillsdale College in Michigan, where two days earlier they had begun a conference on the Second World War. On Sunday night, the noted historian Stephen Ambrose argued that the 21st century would be the greatest and most peaceful in history because of the victory won by the "greatest generation." If other speakers were not quite as optimistic, the mood was still upbeat. Iwo Jima, Guadalcanal, Omaha Beach, still vivid to those who flew those skies and stormed those beaches, will forever remind us of the price that was paid for our freedom. Evil had been routed out in those days. This would be a good century. Then came Tuesday.

After years of planning and enormous expense, blind hate executed an assault on the World Trade Center in New York. It took exactly one hour and 44 minutes after the first attack for the collapse of the Twin Towers.

"I don't know what the gates of hell look like," said John Maloney, a security director for an Internet firm, "but it's got to look like this."[2]

Rudy Guiliani — inspiring, emotional and as tough as ever — rushed to the scene at 8:45. The intrepid mayor of New York described the horror: "When I was looking up, I could see a man just dive out of a window like he was diving into a pool. He came down the full hundred stories and then his fall was broken by the plaza. I think that was the first time I realized that this was beyond anything we had ever faced before."[3]

Marketing executive Kevin Burns said, "I have a photographic image in my brain of the people falling from the sky. I pray."

Fred Golba, a relief worker whose expertise is finding corpses, called the burning Twin Towers "Hell One" and "Hell Two." The picture he paints is not pretty: ". . . jagged glass, girders, the holes go down for stories and you look in and here's all these pieces of people."[4]

Minutes after the towers were struck, United Flight 73 slammed into the Pentagon. "What was that?" Donald Rumsfeld asked. The defense secretary, working in his office somewhere in that building, posed the question we're all asking, what was that? Never in history had a hijacker deliberately flown a plane into a building killing everyone aboard including himself.

What was that? What's going on here? Can anyone by searching find rhyme or reason in this? Has a clash of civilizations threatened the end of history? Why do things like this happen to ordinary folks on their way to college or work, taking their children to school, going about their business?

Brian Sweeney, 38, a passenger on American Airlines Flight 175, had called his wife: "I hope I can call you again, but if not, I want you to have fun. I want you to live your life. I know I'll see you again someday."[5] Minutes later his plane crashed into the South Tower.

A mother heard this message on her answering machine: "Mom, don't worry. A plane hit the World Trade Center. We are going to evacuate. Now pray for us."[6]

Madeline Amy Sweeney, a flight attendant, was calm almost to the end of a call to her supervisor, until she looked out the window and cried, "I see water and buildings! Oh, my God! Oh, my God!"[7]

A team of 62 firefighters, police officers, medical experts, and other rescue specialists from Tacoma, Washington, went to New York to look for survivors and victims. Some of them kept diaries which provide a close-up look at what went on when hell was in session.

"There is anxiety in the air today," therapist Lynn Cheshire writes. "Something has shifted. We discover later it is no longer search and rescue. It is recovery."[8]

Without warning, the current of life is short-circuited. A phone call in the night changes your world forever. A careening car out of control or a violent and angry storm, and the party is suddenly over. Planes crash, dreams unravel, jobs disappear, friends depart. Some images are so vivid they remain unsoftened by the passage of time. You play them over and over.

Six astronauts and a schoolteacher emerging from their quarters, moving briskly, smiling, waving. A van takes them to the launch pad where they are packed away for their journey to the stars.

Seventy-three seconds after liftoff the $1.2 billion space shuttle *Challenger* explodes into a searing nightmare. "What are we doing here? We're reaching for the stars,"[9] schoolteacher Christa McAuliffe said upon entering the astronaut program; but on January 28, 1986, the world watched in horror as seven Americans disappeared in a ball of flames nine miles above the Atlantic.

Our collective grief was expressed in Buenos Aires where Dobal omitted his usual cartoon in the *Clarin* to write, "I can't give you a joke because, dear reader, all my space is filled with infinite pain."

It is a broken world, after all. We walk by faith, not by sight, and have here no continuing city. Our vision is often clouded, and we see through a glass darkly. We have this treasure in earthen vessels and are hard pressed on every side, perplexed, persecuted, struck down, carrying about in the body grim reminders of our mortality.

Who can forget the magnificent voice of Frank Sinatra belting out one of his favorites, "That's Life"? That's life — an apt characterization of the sum total of human experience. The full spectrum of emotions and experiences. The highs and the lows. The warm sensation of success and the cold feeling of failure. Public acclaim and exquisite pleasure; public loss and private pain.

Charles Allen says, "One does not have to live very long in order to find out that life can be hard and cruel — and sometimes almost impossible."[10]

Even as I write, I am deeply moved. How could anyone not be? The experience is something akin to agitation. I run the gamut of feelings until I am tired of running. Sometimes it is anger; white-knuckled, fist-pounding anger, and I echo the sentiment of television personality Danuta Soderman. Early in her life she sought in vain for an answer concerning her career: "I went out to the beach and started walking up and down the shoreline, screaming my rage into the sky. 'Enough! Do you hear me up there? I say enough! I don't want any more of your hope! If you can't come through on your promises, then don't dangle hope in my face. I can't take any more of it! Just leave me alone. . . .'"

At other times it is frustration, the emotion so strong you almost break out in a sweat.

Beneath it all, like a current that never stops, is an abiding sense of deep sadness and loss. When the angry sky clears and the storm subsides and the shouting is muted to a whisper, the question is but a syllable and repeated with only the effort it takes to exhale, Why?

Endnote
1. *Newsweek* (December 3, 2001).
2. *Newsweek* (September 24, 2001).
3. *Newsweek* (December 3, 2001).
4. *Newsweek* (December 1, 2001).
5. Newsweek (December 3, 2001).
6. Ibid.
7. Ibid.
8. *The News Tribune* (Tacoma, WA, October 11, 2001).
9. "Christa McAuliffe 1948-1986," *Time* magazine (February 10, 1986).
10. http://www.faithquest.info/questions/10-why-does-god-allow-suffering-and-evil.

My soul is a dark ploughed

field in the cold rain;

my soul is a broken field

ploughed by pain

(Sara Teasdale, 1884–1933)

CHAPTER TWO

THE PROBLEM OF PAIN

I t's not fair," we cried, when my father lay dying, too weak to move about, hurting, often weeping. As great a Christian as we would ever know, he was a gentle man, modest, self-effacing, of impeccable character and deep conviction. Sixty-two years in the ministry, faithful intercessor, fervent preacher, intrepid pioneer, and zealous church builder.

A family friend once commented, "The Reverend Johnson is the sort of fellow who communicates Christ even when he stands quietly in a corner. The presence of Christ is so powerful in his life it cannot be covered. Just to shake his hand and share a few moments of casual conversation is to be ministered to."

"It's not fair," we cried, when this defenseless man fell victim to a malevolent disease which sprang out of hell (and hell will pay!). Unlike lightning, which strikes a tree, leaving it denuded and bare, this disease, possessed of devils, void of pity and bereft of sympathy, strips the tree one leaf at a time. It can't be abrupt like a falling sword or swift like a descending storm. It is not enough to destroy, it must mock and taunt and torment and humiliate until a strong man cries for relief.

A few years ago my father visited an old friend who was dying of cancer. "The room was filled with the glory of God," Dad said, and his eyes flashed as he described the wonderful presence of the Lord. It was not like that when my father died. There was the embarrassment and humiliation of a body that didn't work, the inability to care for Mother and reluctance to leave her alone. There was weakness and frustration, parched throat and dimming vision — and always the pain.

"Not fair," we cried, "not fair!"

We are confounded by the unevenness of life, perplexed by its disparity — its beauty and pleasure marred by ugliness and pain.

I wrestle with these things as I write in my small second-floor room. On a clear day, Mount Rainier is visible from my window. Although we are separated by a distance of 60 miles, it appears almost close enough to touch.

Something of the charm of this splendid mountain, which rises proudly 14,410 feet, is described in a colorful brochure prepared by the National Park Service: "On a clear day, one can see the peak's snow fields from a distance of over 100 miles. The mind rebels at the idea that an object so distant and yet so much above intervening peaks can be anything more substantial than a cloud formation. But when the cloud refuses to dissipate and remains alone in the sky, the mind evaluates the possibilities and then, suddenly admits to the fact of Mount Rainier."

In a 1915 article written for *The Mountaineer*, Bailey Willis, Stanford University Professor of Geology and member of the Northern Transcontinental Survey, wrote, "I have seen the glories of Switzerland, the grandeur of the Andes, and the grace of the beautiful cone of Fujiyama, but among the most renowned scenery of the world, I know of nothing more majestic or more inspiring than the grandeur of my own old camping ground, Mount Rainier."

But between the little room in which I write and the snow fields of that glorious summit is a cemetery. "Suddenly something happens that sounds like a broken axle in this smoothly rotating machine of life," Helmet Thielcke has said. "We are confronted with a contradiction we simply cannot explain."[1]

A cemetery! Silently mocking the strong and the proud. Sullenly unmindful of broken hearts and human tears. Unresponding to a thousand questions, unyielding to negotiation, beyond bargaining. Supplying no answers, offering no hope, providing no solace. Impartial to age, insensate to logic, oblivious to reason. Unrelenting, unforgiving, unbending. The anguish and pain and grief and loss, unrequited save for the flowers we bring, the birds God sends, and the blessed trees and the grass.

Here beneath low-hanging branches of a tall stately fir lie the bodies of my father and my brother. Over in the corner by the road is the grave of little Amber, five-year-old daughter of special friends, and one recalls Carl Jung's description of the death of a child as a period before the end of a sentence.

"Every time I go to the cemetery," her father says, "I am angry — angry at death! A five-year-old does not belong in the grave. I want to reach down and take her in my arms."

Says David Allan Hubbard, "Death wrenches spirit from flesh with a force and finality that leave us baffled, angry, and fearful. One moment there is a living, breathing, feeling human being by our side, and the next moment there is a pale, still, silent shell."[2]

Death itself is an interloper, an intruder, a thief. Every decent instinct of the human heart recoils from it. When our Lord wept at the tomb of His friend, there was sympathy in those tears, but there was anger as well — anger at "death which virtually always catches us in mid-sentence, and leaves us with endeavors half done."[3]

But the death of a child! The death of youth! The death of a dream! The cruel irony of circumstances which leaves us baffled and dumb and wondering if there really is "another like ourselves, yet unlike us, back of the great vast mystery of life?"[4]

Mark Twain was convinced that the house of life is empty. "Special providence!" he scoffed. "The phrase nauseates me. God doesn't know that we are here, and would not care if He did."[5]

Clive Staples Lewis was born in Belfast, November 29, 1898. His mother died of cancer when he was nine and he was shuffled from one boarding school to another. What little religious faith he possessed disappeared under the dreary tutelage of heavy-handed teachers, one of whom was later certified as insane.

Under the influence of a stern but warm-hearted professor, his atheism was confirmed and, estranged from God, he began a life-long pursuit of medieval and renaissance literature.

The conversion of C.S. Lewis is recounted in *Surprised by Joy*, and during World War II and beyond, he exerted a powerful influence for Christ through his teaching, radio talks, voluminous writings and private life.

The maze of questions elicited by human suffering, which had reinforced his atheism, had to be dealt with when he acknowledged the existence of God and the reality of Jesus Christ. Lewis does so succinctly and eloquently in *The Problem of Pain*, first published in 1940. "If God were good," Lewis writes, "He would wish to make His creatures happy, and if God were almighty, He would be able to do what He wished. But the creatures are not happy. Therefore God lacks either goodness, or power, or both."[6]

Rabbi Harold Kushner finds a partial solution by introducing a limited God. In his best seller, *When Bad Things Happen to Good People*, he suggests that the Lord God may be as perplexed as we are about the mess we're in, suggesting further that we forgive Him for being less than perfect.[7]

To those of us whose God is high and lifted up, almighty and sovereign, such reasoning is unacceptable. Our God is good. He is almighty, and quite able to do what He wishes. Still, the creatures are not happy. Does God therefore lack goodness, or power, or both?

That, my friend, plain and simple, is the problem of pain. It comes in a thousand shapes and sizes and appears in a variety of manifestations. It goes by different names: sickness, fear, loneliness, disappointment, rejection, ridicule, ungrateful children and neglectful children—not to mention the experience of raw unrelenting physical pain and the ultimate encounter with death.

To untangle the web, to sort through the maze, to pursue the "truth," may not be altogether satisfying. Some of the answers may seem inadequate, and for some of the questions there are no answers at all.

Meanwhile, where is God?

Endnotes
  1. Helmet Thielcke, *How the World Began* (James Clarke and Co., 1964), p. 171.
  2. David Allen Hubbard, *Why Do I Have to Die?* (Ventura, CA: Regal Books, 1978).
  3. Ibid., p. 45.

4. James Wallace Hamilton, *Who Goes There? What and Where Is God?* (Grand Rapids, MI: Fleming H. Revell, 1958), p. 11.
5. Ibid., p. 13.
6. C.S. Lewis, *The Problem of Pain* (New York: Macmillan, 1962).
7. Harold S. Kushner, *When Bad Things Happen to Good People* (New York: Avon Books, 1981).

Far more crucial than
what we know or do not
know is what we do not
want to know.

(Eric Hoffer, 1902–1983)

CHAPTER THREE
WHEN YOU
ASK WHY

W hy? Just why?" The question came
from a man of devout faith, with a
serious turn of mind and sensitive spirit. "I
don't understand why God let Ron die," he
said.

I had some concern that this man's faith
might be undermined. If God failed this
time, could one be sure of anything, even
saving faith?

It did seem like a pointless tragedy.
Ronald R. Redlich had two earned degrees,
one in business administration, the other in
engineering. Handsome, bright, consider-
ate, committed to Christ, devoted to people,
recently engaged to be married; now the victim of a burning fever that raged like a fire
through his brain, ravaging his body, leaving
it wasted and spent — dead at the age of 27.

"In the first place," I replied to my troubled friend, "when you ask why, you're not alone.

"Look at Jacob," I went on. "His son Joseph had long been gone; dead, he thought. Now they were taking Benjamin, his baby boy. 'All these things are against me,' he lamented (Gen. 42:36).

"Question marks punctuate the Psalms: 'Why do You stand so far off, O Lord? Why do You hide yourself in times of trouble?' (Ps. 10:1). 'Why are you cast down, O my soul? And why are you disquieted in me?' (Ps. 42:5).

"Listen to the moaning of Job: 'Why did I not die in the womb?' (Job 3:11). 'Why have You sent me as a mark against You, so that I am a burden to myself?' (Job 7:20).

"And was ever a question as poignant as that which came from the Cross, when the Son of God cried, 'My God, my God, why have You forsaken me?'

"Nor is it wrong to question," I continued. "God can take care of Himself. Far from discouraging our probing, He encourages us in the quest: 'Come now, and let us reason together,' He says (Isa. 1:18).

"When Job's world tumbled in, he sought an answer. He said, 'The cause which I knew not I searched out' (Job 29:16). He didn't confuse piety with mental inertia.

"Some answers are not forthcoming," I admitted. "There is a reason for everything, though many of the reasons are not disclosed."

A young lady who had suffered a crippling accident made a sensible statement: "One of the first things you learn is that some questions don't have answers."

There are more than 300 questions in the Book of Job and most of them are never answered. The problem haunts us throughout life. Someone wrote Billy Graham and asked, "I've never understood something about God. If God is supposed to be good, where did evil come from?"

The fact that Harold Kushner's book, *When Bad Things Happen to Good People*, became an instant best seller, may reflect man's yearning for answers, his search for satisfying solutions.

One thing is certain: human suffering is not alleviated by resorting to trite and shallow answers. Why add to the agony of a broken heart the burden of empty words? Talk is often cheap, but foolish talk is always costly.

It is amazing how entrenched are certain views, many of which are pagan philosophies. To stand in the face of stark tragedy and piously avow, "Whatever comes, God's will is done," is to fly in the face of reason and adopt the thinking of knaves.

Fatalism is a philosophy for pagans, not a credo for Christians. The doctrine is derived from heathenism, with no moral support in the Word of God. It was conceived by the enemy, spawned in hell, articulated by the worldly wise, and pawned off on unsuspecting souls as a teaching worthy of acceptance. It is not.

Other faulty formulations define human suffering as proof of God's love; insist upon our entering into Christ's suffering as co-redemptive with His own (fallen man finds it hard to accept the free gift of God's grace); or suggest some twisted logic: "Look how much this or that person suffered; why should I escape?"

To reject the validity of these bank-rupt and tired tenets is not to deny the fact that there are causes for the suffering we see.

It is instructive to note that the first question in the Bible was posed by Satan. It came with a sneer: "Has God indeed said, 'You shall not eat of every tree of the garden?' " (Gen. 3:1). There were no questions before the enemy came, but we've been staggered by them ever since.

Many of the tragedies in the world today are a direct result of sin, and there is no need to look further for answers, to speculate, to question — or to blame God.

Sin is here. The earth is cursed, and because of it the whole creation groans and travails. The blood of Abel cries from the ground. The very planet reels under the weight of this burden, and there is no way to understand the human condition apart from the fact of sin.

Sin is alien to God's creation. It spoiled earth's pristine beauty and has sullied every succeeding age. The very planet is defiled, every blade of grass marked. "We shall never understand our age," an American theologian reminds us, "if we do not comprehend the principle in which we see Satan attacking the people of God."[1]

For reasons known only to himself, God has chosen to give man considerable freedom. Why? Perhaps a clue is to be found in the reasoned argument of Donald Grey Barnhouse: "The universe should see, once and for all, if it were possible for any creature whatsoever, of any rank, however exalted, to live for even a moment independent of God the Creator . . . so that it might be demonstrated that nothing good could ever come to the creation apart from that which originates in God himself."[2]

The gift of freedom, both precious and awesome, must be taken into account in any serious study of the problem of suffering.

Having acknowledged the direct link between sin and suffering, between man's disobedience and his pain, we are primarily concerned with the large tragedies and small discomforts cluttering the landscape of life which are beyond definition, beyond explanation and beyond understanding.

C.S. Lewis was a confirmed bachelor until his mid-fifties when he met and married an American poet, Joy Davidman Gresham. They lived together four exquisite years and, although stricken with cancer before their marriage, her death left Lewis totally devastated. *A Grief Observed* records the jottings of his grief on pages from his diary written during those days. A poignant line appears early in the small volume: "Meanwhile, where is God?"[3]

Having brought God into the equation, other questions arise: "Who is God?" and "What kind of a God is He?"

A.W. Tozer makes a profound observation: "What comes into our minds when we think about God is the most important thing about us."[4]

GOD IS GOOD

There is a God, and He is good. The enemy induced Eve to question God's essential goodness, and we've been doing it ever since. We blame Him for accidents, misfortune, tragedies. Whatever our theological persuasions, and however difficult life's problems may be, let us not malign God. It is the character of a thief to steal, to kill, and to destroy. It is the nature of God to give, forgive, heal, and restore. Wherever the gospel goes, the lot of man improves. It is God's business to save and to help, to lift up.

God does not cause the tragedy and terror that stalk the earth. He allows it, and He employs it for our good; but He does not cause it, nor is it His will.

Former U.S. Senate Chaplain Richard C. Halverson said, "It may be difficult to explain how a God of love could allow the terrible agony, suffering, and tragedy in the world, but it is infinitely more difficult to explain these facts of life and leave God out of the picture."

The character, intention, and love of God were never more accurately depicted than on that day long ago when a Cross was planted on a hill outside the walls of Jerusalem. There, by a great highway, the Savior was crucified. There God was in Christ reconciling the world unto Himself. On that Cross, as throughout His earthly ministry, Jesus set himself against sin, disease, poverty, fear, and death.

"What then shall we say to these things? If God is for us, who can be against us?" (Romans 8:31).

God is *for* you! Believe that!

GOD IS ALL-KNOWING

The fact that God knows everything was a source of comfort to Oral and Evelyn Roberts when tragedy struck in their lives. Early on a Saturday morning, a friend came to their home. He opened the newspaper and showed them the story of a plane crash. "We think it's Marshall and Rebecca," he said. Rebecca was the oldest of the four Roberts children and Marshall was her husband. Returning from a skiing trip in Colorado, they had crashed in a wheat field in Kansas. Another couple died as well.

Their first concern was for the children, now orphaned. They immediately dressed and prepared to drive across town to where the children were being care for. While they were driving, Oral Roberts said, "My first word was 'Why? Why has this happened to me? What have I done to deserve it? This is our oldest daughter, precious daughter, and precious son-in-law. Why?' And then the Lord brought this to my heart, *God must know something about this we don't know.*"

Look at Job — he never knew what hit him. Or why. He lived his entire life unaware of the drama going on in the heavens.

The Bible says that Job was "the greatest of all the people in the East." He had great possessions: seven thousand sheep, three thousand camels, five hundred yoke of oxen, five hundred female donkeys, and a very large household.

He was a devout man, loyal husband, faithful father. He rose early in the morning to offer burnt offerings for his children. But there came a day (Job 1:6) when Satan presented himself before the Lord. He accused Job of serving God for gain. He charged him with "commercial faith" — *He's in this for what he can get out of it.* Satan maligned Job's character, his motives.

When given permission to try the poor man, Satan unleashed the forces of nature. Job lost his family, his possessions and his health — and he never knew what hit him.

Job was unaware of the contest in heaven, but God knew — and Job trusted God.

GOD IS PURPOSEFUL

The purposes of suffering are clearly stated in the Word of God:

> My brethren, count it all joy when you fall into various trials, knowing that the testing of your faith produces patience (James 1:2–3).

> Beloved, do not think it strange concerning the fiery trial which is to try you, as though some strange thing happened to you; but rejoice to the extent that you partake of Christ's sufferings, that when His glory is revealed, you may also be glad with exceeding joy (1 Pet. 4:12–13).

Development of character and growth in grace are often the result of positive response to pressure at some point in our lives. "Now no chastening seems to be joyful for the present, but painful," Paul writes, "nevertheless, afterward it yields the peaceable fruit of righteousness to those who have been trained by it" (Heb. 12:11).

Dr. Paul Tournier was a general practitioner in Geneva for nearly 50 years. Without special training, and disdaining the title of psychiatrist, he came to develop and practice what he called "medicine of the person." Many patients, he came to believe, needed help going deeper than drugs or surgery. His keen insight is illustrated in one of his books when he speaks of the blessings of a deep loss: "The greater the grief, the greater the creative energy to which it gives rise."[5]

Sometimes we are forced to grow, and "the whole purpose of life is to grow," Dr. Robert R. Carkhuff writes in his excellent book, *The Art of Helping*. "We are born with the potential to grow — no more — no less! From the moment we enter the world to the instant we exit this life, we experience opportunities for growth."[6]

God permitted Job to suffer in order to silence Satan. Former pastor and prolific author Warren Wiersbe made a striking observation when he wrote: "By the way, have you ever stopped to consider that Job paid a great price for you and me? Because he lost everything, and by his suffering proved Satan wrong, you and I don't have to lose everything. God can test us on a much smaller scale because the battle against Satan's lie has now been won by God."[7]

Disappointment and pain have a way of weaning us away from this world. Joni Eareckson Tada writes in *A Step Further*, "Suffering gets us ready for heaven. How does it get us ready? It makes us want to go there. Broken necks, broken arms, broken bones, broken hearts — these things crush our illusions that earth can keep its promises. When we come to know that the hopes we cherished will never come true, that our loved one is gone from this life forever, that we will never be as pretty, popular, successful, or famous as we had once imagined, it lifts our sights. It moves our eyes from this world, which God knows could never satisfy us anyway, and sets them on the life to come. Heaven becomes our passion."[8]

A friend and I agonized over a difficult situation. "When we get to heaven," I volunteered, "we'll ask the Lord about it."

"When we get to heaven, it won't make any difference," my friend replied.

In his little book, *Inward Ho*, Christopher Morley wrote, "I had a million questions to ask God; but when I met Him, they all fled my mind; and it didn't seem to matter."[9]

Endnotes

1. Donald Grey Barnhouse, *The Invisible War* (Grand Rapids, MI: Zondervan, 1965), p. 108.
2. Ibid.
3. C.S. Lewis, *A Grief Observed* (San Francisco, CA: Harper, 1989).
4. A.W. Tozer, *The Knowledge of the Holy* (New York: HarperCollins, 1978), p. 1.
5. Paul Tournier, *Creative Suffering* (San Francisco, CA: Harper & Row, 1981).
6. Robert R. Carkhuff, *The Art of Helping* (Amherst, MA: Human Resource Development Press, 1993).
7. Warren Wiersbe, *Why Us? When Bad Things Happen to God's People* (Grand Rapids, MI: Baker Book House, 1984).

8. Steve Estes and Joni Eareckson, *A Step Further* (Grand Rapids, MI: Zondervan Publishing House, 1978).
9. Christopher Morley, *Inward Ho* (Garden City, NY: Doubleday, Page & Co., 1923).

A suffering person does
not need a lecture — he
needs a listener.[1]

(Billy Graham, 1918–)

CHAPTER FOUR
BEYOND UNDERSTANDING

The Christian faces life head-on. Christianity does not gloss over reality. The Scriptures are clear concerning the true character of life, and human experience bears it out. "Trouble is not an interruption in life," Bruce Barton said, "it is the stuff of which life is made."

I remember standing at the bedside of a young man who was dying. We asked the usual questions, cornered the doctor and plied the nurses with queries — when suddenly it hit me: What are explanations when your heart is breaking? Who cares how the young man contracted the dreaded disease? The pity is that he has it. What is the meaning of this endless litany of verbiage — definitions, analysis, explanations? What is the value of our recently acquired medical expertise? So we have become overnight experts in a disease called encephalitis; we can even spell it. Our vocabulary is weighted with words unknown to us a fortnight ago. Death is the same from any cause. But is there a balm in Gilead? Is there a physician here?

Former pastor and prolific author Warren Wiersbe said, "God is not standing at the end of a syllogism, nor is peace of mind found at the conclusion of an argument."[2]

The apostle Paul was writing from a Roman prison when he penned these words:

> Rejoice in the Lord always.
> Again I will say, rejoice! Let your
> gentleness be known to all men.
> The Lord is at hand. Be anxious for
> nothing, but in everything by prayer
> and supplication, with thanksgiving,
> let your requests be made known to
> God; and the peace of God, which
> surpasses all understanding, will
> guard your hearts and minds through
> Christ Jesus (Phil. 4:4–7).

A broken heart yearns for revelation rather than explanation. It is God we need, a sense of His presence. Beyond understanding are peace, hope, trust, and ultimate triumph at last.

PEACE

This is the peace of God. It is strikingly different from the world's concept of peace. Jesus said, "Peace I leave with you, My peace I give you; not as the world gives do I give to you. Do not let your heart be troubled, neither let it be afraid" (John 14:27).

One writer observed that this peace "covers every single relationship in life. It captures the Old Testament *shalom*. It carries into the New Testament the concept of that ideal state of life — wholeness, well-being, harmony. It embodies a totality of life that is available when a person is right with God."[3]

The peace of God passes all human understanding. It is not determined by material gain or affected by material loss. It can be present in the most violent storm, in the heart of conflict and crisis, in the darkest night. There is no finer testimony than this quality of life when no earthly reason exists for its presence.

The Sunday before announcing my resignation in Milwaukee, a neighboring pastor called and said, "Dan, I have a verse of Scripture for you — Jeremiah 29:11. Let me read it to you: 'For I know the thoughts that I think toward you says the LORD, thoughts of peace and not of evil, to give you a future and a hope.'"

A few days later, speaking at a school for preachers, that verse was again brought to my attention. In a chapel service, the song leader paused between stanzas of a hymn and said, "Some of us in this room are in a time of transition; our lives are changing. I want to read a verse of Scripture which speaks to our condition." And he read Jeremiah 29:11.

I remembered that somewhere in the Bible it says that in the mouth of two or three witnesses a thing shall be established.

Three weeks after arriving at Heritage USA, we drove down to take possession of our new house. It was the day after the startling announcement at PTL. In the mailbox was a letter from our daughter in Memphis. Included in the envelope was a card on which were printed these words: "For I know the thoughts that I think toward you, says the Lord, thoughts of peace and not of evil, to give you a future and a hope."

Three times that promise was given to us. A coincidence? Perhaps. Or was it the Lord's way of preparing us for what lay ahead?

There is a peace which passes understanding, which surpasses logic. It has nothing to do with man's wisdom — it has everything to do with the promises of a sovereign God who has promised to keep him in perfect peace, whose mind is stayed on Him.

HOPE

Hope was born in my soul when I was a small boy. Half a century ago, on a night I still remember, I lay in bed thinking and crying. My father was the pastor of a little church in North Dakota. We lived in crowded quarters behind the small auditorium. Mother and Dad slept downstairs and the boys shared an upstairs attic bedroom. Everyone was asleep, or so I thought.

The house was quiet, except for my crying. When Dad heard me, he came upstairs and knelt by my bed. "What's wrong?" he asked.

"Daddy," I said, "I was just thinking how terrible it would be if you died and left us alone."

My father took my hands in his and said, "Maybe we'll never die; maybe Jesus will come and we'll all go to heaven together."

My heart wrapped its fingers around that hope and I fell asleep. I slept through the night and have lived through the years with the hope that Jesus might come before death does.

Dad grew old and I grew up and our perspectives are different now, but the hope remains, its light undimmed. Paul writes:

> But I do not want you to be ignorant, brethren, concerning those who are asleep, lest you sorrow as

others who have no hope. For if
we believe that Jesus died and rose
again, even so God will bring with
Him those who sleep in Jesus. For
this we say by the word of the Lord,
that we who are alive and remain until the coming of the Lord will by no
means precede those who are asleep.
For the Lord himself will descend
from heaven with a shout, with the
voice of an archangel, and with the
trumpet of God. And the dead in
Christ will rise first. Then we who
are alive and remain shall be caught
up together with them in he clouds
to meet the Lord in the air. And thus
we shall always be with the Lord.
Therefore comfort one another with
these words (1 Thess. 4:13–18).

I know of a pastor who once lived about
half a mile from the Farragut National
Academy. On clear days when they paraded,
he said he could hear distinctly the music
of the academy band. On some days, however, when the south wind blew softly in

the opposite direction, he could hear only the thumping of the big bass drum. Yet on those days, he said, when he couldn't hear the whole band, he knew it was there. He knew there was more than the pounding of a drum.

Because we know that in all things God is at work for our good, we are confident that storms are not forever, the sky will clear again. Somewhere the band is playing — there's more than the pounding of the drum. Somewhere the sun is shining, and it will outlast all the clouds of all the centuries.

TRUST

We can afford to trust if we are rightly related to the Lord. This truth is graphically portrayed in the beautiful metaphor of the potter and the clay in Jeremiah 18: "Then I went down to the potter's house, and there he was, making something at the wheel. And the vessel that he made of clay was marred in the hand of the potter; so he made it again into another vessel, as it seemed good to the potter to make" (Jer. 18:3–4).

The vessel was marred *in* the potter's hand. *What* happens — and *why,* are of less importance than *where!* Where are we? We are in the potter's hand!

Vance Havner told the following story. During the London blitz of World War II many children were evacuated to the country by order of the government. As one load pulled out, someone asked a youngster, "Where are you going?"

"I don't know," he replied, "but the king knows."

Havner commented, "I don't know where I'm headed or what lies out there, but my King knows, and I have one ambition left, to be His faithful subject."[4]

But who is this God who is good, who is all-knowing, who acts with deliberate purpose — this stranger who leaves footprints on the shores of the unknown? An African chief said, "We know at night that somebody goes among the trees, but we never speak of it."

Jesus gave this somebody a name. He called him Father, and you can afford to trust Him.

Simply trusting everyday,
Trusting through a stormy way;
Even when my faith is small,
Trusting Jesus that is all.[5]

Endnotes

1. Franklin Graham with Donna Lee Toney, *Billy Graham in Quotes* (Nashville, TN: Thomas Nelson, 2011), p. 334.
2. Warren Wiersbe, *Why Us? When Bad Things Happen to God's People* (Grand Rapids, MI: Fleming H. Revell, 1985), p. 13.
3. Rev. Eli Klingensmith, "Prince of Peace," 12/20/2009, http://www.docstoc.com/docs/37129159/Prince-of-Peace.
4. Vance Havner, *Though I Walk Through the Valley* (Old Tappen, NJ: Fleming H. Revell, 1974).
5. "Trusting Jesus," lyrics by Edgar Page Stites.

I shall not live 'til I see God;

and when I have seen Him,

I shall never die.

(John Donne, 1572–1631)

CHAPTER FIVE
DEALING WITH GRIEF

It was 7:30 on a Monday morning. We were in a motel in Grand Island, Nebraska, when the phone rang. We knew my father was dying and the call was not totally unexpected. We were heading home, would arrive in two days, but it was not soon enough.

"Do you want to talk to Mother?" my brother asked.

"Yes, I do," I replied.

When Mother took the phone, she said, "Hello, Daniel."

"Hi, Mama, so Father is gone."

"Yes," she said, "and today is our 61st wedding anniversary."

I was suddenly aware of the unpredictability of one's responses. "The most common problem in grief is not knowing what reactions to expect from oneself," it has been observed.[1]

The Presbyterian pastor Donald Grey Barnhouse said he was totally unprepared when news came that his mother had died. "Like a flash of lightning that leaves a scar down the side of a tree, the news was upon me," he said.[2]

"No one ever told me that grief felt so like fear," C.S. Lewis wrote after the death of his wife. "I am not afraid, but the sensation is like being afraid. The same fluttering in the stomach, the same restlessness, the yawning. I keep on swallowing. . . . I dread the moments when the house is empty. If only they would talk to one another and not to me."[3]

Paul Tournier comments on his responses to his wife's death: "Ah! Growing old alone is quite different from growing old together! What I miss most is the rich dialogue that existed between us."[4]

UNDERSTANDING GRIEF

Grief is a normal response to an event which runs counter to what we think life should be. Doug Manning wrote, "Grieving is as natural as crying when you are hungry. . . . It is nature's way of healing a broken heart."[5]

Shakespeare believed that "everyone can master a grief but he that has it." Like the other person's toothache, it is easy to philosophize, to speculate, but not as easy to understand, let alone sympathize. The heart knows its own bitterness, and the valley of the shadow of death is best defined by those who have been there.

There is a fellowship of suffering, a fraternity of the brokenhearted. Joe and Linda Ellis were drawn into that fellowship on a Monday afternoon five years ago. At three o'clock, Joe called his five-year-old daughter on the telephone. Thirty minutes later her body lay lifeless in the front seat of the family car, color book and crayons strewn around. It was a cruel, freak accident — and Amber will always be five.

"Grief is something you live with," Joe told me. "You see a little girl in a restaurant, hands reaching to the top of the counter, her nose pressed against the glass. Something about her hair, her height, the wistful look at an item in the counter — and the wound is raw again. It's like an ambush."

"Every anniversary, every memory, every comparison brings the loved one to the hospital bed and the open grave," observed a reluctant member of the fraternity of the brokenhearted.

A caring and sensitive Portland, Oregon, woman developed a school for children who have lost a parent. The instruction, lessons, and therapy extend over a period of several weeks. Upon completion of the course, before leaving for home, each child is given a handful of stones, all of them smooth but one. The smooth stones are a reminder of pleasant memories and good times, and a symbol that healing has begun. The single rough stone is a reminder that the loss is never completely forgotten.

Five stages of grief are identified in the book *Happiness Is a Choice* by Frank B. Minirth and Paul Meier. The first is *denial*. One simply refuses to believe.[6] The second stage is *anger turned outward*. This is anger directed toward someone other than ourselves. It is sometimes experienced by a young child when losing a parent due to death or divorce. It may be directed toward God.

This is followed by *anger turned inward*. At this stage one blames himself for some real or imagined wrong. There may be a deep hostility, a grudge. According to the authors, the next stage is *genuine grief*. This is a necessary phase and should not be suppressed. Eugenia Price suggests that grief is to be lived through, not mastered. "However," she says, "we dare not permit grief to master us."

Resolution is the fifth and final step, and after three to six weeks one may begin to regain some zest for life.

Our oldest brother died suddenly, and much too soon, we thought. My father was distraught, unsteady on his feet, sometimes driving erratically. Several days after the funeral, he surprised the younger ministers at church by striding resolutely into a staff meeting and declaring, "Well, I've buried my boy, now it's time to get back to work."

DEALING WITH GRIEF

If grief is a process, something you have to work your way through, how do you deal with it? How do you handle the variety of emotions, the physical and mental stress, the loneliness, the unexpected loss of friends? What positive steps can be taken when you feel like Job must have felt when he lamented, "Oh, that my grief were fully weighed, and my calamity laid with it on the scales! For then it would be heavier than the sand of the sea" (Job 6:2–3).

Accept the loss. Come to terms with it. Try to understand what's happening. Be prepared for a journey through the wilderness. Don't be surprised if friends disappoint you. Some will disappear. "My relatives have failed, and my close friends have forgotten," Job cried. "Those who dwell in my house, and my maidservants, count me as a stranger; I am an alien in their sight. . . . I am repulsive to the children of my own body. Even young children despise me" (Job 19:14–18).

Be prepared for a rough ride, but couple that with a determination to survive and a refusal to get locked into one or another of the stages of the process. Keep moving. Resist surrender. Avoid isolation. Face up to life. Somebody needs you. You're not alone. You must live again, live fully again!

Remember. Put your thinking cap on. Use your mind. A wise counselor suggests the value of "deliberately taking memory trips to places and events connected to your relationship with the person now gone. Think through every facet of the relationship."

Over lunch, Joe Ellis spoke freely about his five-year-old, answering questions, volunteering insights. We had met in a restaurant on the shore of the Puget Sound. The sky was cloudless that day, the water shimmering and still. Anderson Island lay in the distance and the mountains beyond. "This was Amber's favorite restaurant," Joe said. "She loved to come here. We were here the Sunday before she died.

"I'll never forget that day," my friend remembered, growing wistful. His eyes reflected pain and pleasure as he said, "she wanted so badly to come. I told her we'd better not this time; it did cost quite a bit.

She cried — and we came. I'll always be glad we did."

A pleasant memory is warm, like the hugs of a two-year-old, comforting like a "soft pillow for a tired heart," a thing of beauty to be admired like a precious stone you hold in your hand and turn round and round.

Record your journey. When you have thought yourself full, write yourself empty. Anne Freemantle makes an interesting observation about the value of writing. Referring to *A Grief Observed* by C.S. Lewis, she says, "The author has done something I had believed impossible—assuaged his own grief by conveying it."[7]

This is what the Psalmist did — and that's why we love the Psalms. They are replete with charges, accusations, questions; every human emotion: joy, sorrow, even anger. Listen:

> How long, O LORD? Will you forget me forever? How long will You hide Your face from me? How long shall I take counsel in my soul,

having sorrow in my heart daily? How long will my enemy be exalted over me? (Ps. 13:1–2). My God, my God, why have You forsaken me? Why are You so far from helping Me, and from the words of My groaning? O my God, I cry in the daytime, but You do not hear; and in the night season, and am not silent (Ps. 22:1–2). Rejoice in the LORD, O you righteous! For praise from the upright is beautiful. Praise the LORD with the harp; make melody to Him with an instrument of ten strings. Sing to Him a new song; play skillfully with a shout of joy (Ps. 33:1–3).

Following are two examples of how I assuaged my own grief "by conveying it."

COACH OR FIRST CLASS

In my business, Sunday morning always finds me in church. There are rare exceptions. This is one of them. I am calling United Airlines for a flight to Seattle, Washington. There's a departure at 3:45

this afternoon, with layover and change in Denver, arriving on the West Coast at 8:10 tonight.

"Coach or first class?" a friendly voice asks.

"Coach," I reply.

A brief pause is followed by confirmation: "I have a reservation for you on Flight 248 leaving Milwaukee at 3:45. May I have your last name please?"

"Johnson," I reply.

"First initial?"

"D," I answer.

"D as in David?" she asks.

"Yes, ma'am, D as in David."

She goes on talking, but I am no longer listening. David is my brother. He died this morning, his life cut short by a sudden and violent stroke. He was 54. There were five boys and one girl in our family. There still are five boys and one girl in our family, but one of the brothers has flown the "friendly skies."

You're wondering whether he went coach or first class. At first, we weren't certain. Departure was sudden and takeoff a little stormy, but when he landed in the Big City, Dave was riding first class.

HOW DO YOU SAY GOODBYE WITHOUT HURTING?

Today we said goodbye. Early this morning, our youngest grandson flew off with his mother. His father had left by car two days earlier. The moving van is somewhere in between, and Seattle lies in the distance.

Austin David was born in Little Rock two years ago. He came with dimples — the one on the right side is deeper than the one on the left. He laughs easily and often and we think he's happy to be in the family.

The move cuts short a good thing we had going, he and I. We had a way of communicating with each other the wisdom peculiar to our ages. There was a certain solace in being together, comforted by the thought that the camaraderie would never end.

It's 20 minutes to the airport. The freeway passes County Stadium, Marquette University, and Notre Dame High School. Small talk will help: "See that clock, Cindy?" I ask.

"It's the largest clock of its kind in the world; bigger than Big Ben." She knows the line by heart. It's part of the tour when guests arrive; Wisconsin Bank Building and Grand Avenue Mall, city parks and lake-front drive, botanical gardens and the big clock atop the Allen-Bradley building.

We arrive at the airport, park the car, hurry inside, and find the gate. The flight is called, and they are gone. I fetch dark glasses and am lost in the crowd.

A boy going off to war thought it would be less painful if he and his father separated privately at home rather than publicly at the train depot. After a brief farewell in the pre-dawn darkness, the son turned and walked away, crunching inches of freshly fallen snow, and etching indelibly in the memory of his father the sight of a boy growing smaller and smaller as he appeared and disappeared in the light of the street lamps.

My little brother had a good idea. Years ago, Clayton spent time with a family in western Kansas. He was working and saving for college, and the good family welcomed him as one of their own. Clayton stayed long enough to get attached to the youngsters in the home and dreaded the day he would leave. When the time came to go, he packed his things, drove his car to the back door and began loading. When he had made the last trip, he went to his room, closed the door, opened the window, climbed out, jumped into his car, and drove away.

A cop-out? You're right; Clayton was smart that way.

I recall one of our last visits with Mom and Dad. We crowded every precious minute with movement. We ate and drank, laughed and cried, took pictures and looked at pictures, went to the mountain, had dinner at home, went out for supper, and fell exhausted into bed.

It's midnight, and we must catch an early flight. The departure must be arranged with care. It will help to arrive at the airport with little time to spare. As it turns out, we have no time to spare. The place is crawling with people. Everywhere, lines are long. We have taken advantage of a discount the airline offered; so has everyone else, or so it seems.

We check our bags and pass security only to learn at the gate that the plane is full, overbooked. No matter that we have tickets. The agents explain, apologize, cajole. They offer round-trip tickets to anywhere to passengers who will fly another time.

They offer practically everything except the airline itself. "We'll give you a round-trip ticket to Puerto Rico if you'll give up your seats," they promise.

"But we don't want to go to Puerto Rico," we protest. "We want to go to Milwaukee."

Agents squirm and passengers scheme as we move into the end zone for a touchdown (takeoff). The game plan dictates the strategy: Stand close to the agent; palms open, hands down on the top of the counter. Let her see you. Do not move. Do *not* get angry (you may act a little put out). Repeat, like a recording, "We've got to get on this plane. We've got to get on this plane."

Of course the whole thing is a blessing. The hassle precludes the possibility of the lingering farewell. There just isn't time.

Tennyson wrote, "Thou madest man, he knows not why; he thinks he was not made

to die." He also knows he was not made
to say goodbye. "We've got to get on this
plane," we plead.

"Follow me," an exasperated agent pro-
claims. We grab our things and shout, "See
you, Mom; see you Dad. Too bad we didn't
have more time."

The attendant on board is not happy
to see us, but we are happy, and relieved,
laughing up our sleeves as we jostle our way
down the crowded aisle. We find two seats
in the back by the toilets; but never mind,
we have survived one more parting pretty
well intact.

How do you eliminate the wrenching
pain of parting? Hide red eyes behind black
glasses; exit hastily, no time to get weepy:
"See you, Mom. . . ." Or maybe Clayton was
onto something — climb out the window.

My father once told me that Christians
never say goodbye for the last time. And
Cindy says, "In heaven we'll all live in the
same town." But until we get to the same
town, we have this little problem: How do
you say goodbye without hurting?

You don't. You really don't.

Talk. Upon learning of my father's death, I immediately called an old family friend. When John the Baptist was imprisoned, his disciples came and told Jesus. It is important to share with someone you trust. Kahlil Gibran remarked, "You may forget with whom you laughed, but you will never forget with whom you wept."[8]

> Are you weary, are you heavy hearted?
> Tell it to Jesus, tell it to Jesus.
> Are you grieving over joys departed?
> Tell it to Jesus alone.[9]

Weep. Don't hold back the tears. Crying is a normal and necessary part of the healing process. When British prime minister Winston Churchill learned of the critical and complete loss of Britain's premier warships *HMS Prince of Wales* and the *HMS Repulse* stationed in Singapore, both sunk by Japanese Imperial forces, causing the death of the British Vice Admiral, he closed his door, went to the bureau which contained handkerchiefs, and wrote later, "I was thankful to be alone."

Tears. What are they, and why do they come? Scientists have studied them the way they have studied eyes, ears, nose, throat, bone, marrow, and tissue; but there are many unanswered questions.

We are told that only human beings have the ability to shed tears of sorrow. Doctors believe that weeping may rid the body of chemicals produced in distress. Dr. William H. Frey, a biochemist at St. Paul-Ramsey Medical Center in Minnesota, stated that "tears wept in anguish have a different chemical composition than those shed in response to irritations such as cold, wind, or dust."[10] Frey suggested that stress-related diseases such as peptic ulcers may be aggravated by the suppression of tears. Tears are a sign of compassion, not weakness. There's nothing like "a good cry" to cleanse the wound and hasten the healing process.

Refuse to live in fear. I asked Joe Ellis about this. He and Linda have two other children. "Are you afraid that something might happen to them when they go out?" I asked.

His answer came without hesitation, and revealed a deep faith in God and a good deal of common sense: "Linda and I made a decision not to let Amber's death destroy our lives."

Studies have shown that illness or the death of a child often results in divorce of the parents. A California study revealed that "the marriages of a startling 80 percent of parents with children who had cancer finally broke up."

Doctor Sidney Arje of the American Cancer Society says, "When people find themselves in this situation there are all kinds of reactions. There is a big interplay of aggressions and before you know it, many husbands and wives are chewing one another up."

My friend was familiar with these studies and well aware of the hazards, but again his answer was reasoned and sensible: "We resolved to help bring down the statistics."

They resolutely refuse to live in the shadow of yesterday's sorrow, or be stampeded by panic and swept away in a torrent of fear.

Allow time for healing. The year after Amber's death was particularly trying for her father. Everything seemed to go wrong and his health deteriorated. "I sought out the best cardiologist on the West Coast," he told me. "After careful examination he said, 'Joe, you've got the heart of a horse — it's just broken.' Then he recommended three things: Be sure you eat, and eat properly; get plenty of rest; and engage in big muscle-movement sports.

It is important to remember that healing is a process and that time is required to complete that process. "Human pain does not loosen its grip at one point in time," a discerning writer observed. "Rather, it works its way out of our consciousness over time. There is a season of sadness. A season of anger. A season of tranquility. A season of hope. But these seasons do not follow one another in lockstep manner."[11]

HELPING THE BEREAVED

As we work our way through these seasons of life and find for ourselves the healing balm, we become "wounded healers," and understand what Paul meant when he wrote, "God . . . comforts us in all our tribulation, that we may be able to comfort those who are in any trouble, with the comfort with which we ourselves are comforted by God" (2 Cor. 1:3–4).

The scene is all too familiar. Illness and death are followed by funeral arrangements. Family and friends are called, food is brought in, flowers arrive. Friends across the country and neighbors across the street come or call expressing sympathy and pledging support: "Don't hesitate to call if you need help." "Let us know if we can do anything — anything at all." "We'll get together."

Unfortunately, just when the shock of loss wears off and the pain of reality sets in, the line of comforters narrows to a trickle. Suddenly the house is empty and you are alone. And lonely. What do I do now? Where is everybody?

The picture may be overdrawn, but you'll never know until you're there. It is not that friends do not care — they do not know what to do. They feel awkward. It is one thing to exchange ideas, but to share feelings — that is risky and painful, and it is easer to stay away. There are some things we can do, some positive steps we can take to ease the burden and share the load of those who mourn.

Be available. Be there. Before you talk or pray or bring a hot dish, just be there. Let the bereaved feel your presence. "I don't remember anything that was said," a woman told a friend when her husband died. "What I remember are those heartfelt hugs."

This is no time for sermonettes or breezy conversation. Minutes after Joseph Bayly's five-year-old died of leukemia, the nurse who had attended him found herself on the elevator with Bayly. "I wish I could say something that would help ease your pain," she said.

He replied, "You just did."[12]

Be attentive. Listen. A woman came to my office for counseling. She was in deep trouble and in a moment was pouring out her soul. I had no answer to her questions and did not know how to counsel her.

When she had finished, we had a brief prayer and she rose to leave. Tears filled her eyes as she said, "I can't thank you enough for what you have done. You have really helped me." Except for the prayer, I had not spoken half a dozen words; I had only listened.

In *Don't Take My Grief Away,* Doug Manning writes: "We have never discovered the power of the ear. When someone tells us his or her problems we think we must have an answer. If we have no answer, we feel as though we have been no help at all. The frustration of having no answer can cause us to either give shallow answers or just run from the question."

Manning goes on to say, "The ear is the most powerful part of the human body. People are healed by the laying on of ears. . . . In grief, you need ears."[13]

Be communicative. Engage in constructive conversation. People should be encouraged to talk about what happened. Listen to them, then ask questions if it feels right. How did you feel when that occurred? What happened next? Then what did you do? What did the doctor say?

A mother whose son had died said, "My greatest fear was that my son's life would go unnoticed and unremembered." Joe Ellis echoes a similar concern: "The only way to keep Amber alive is to talk about her. She won't grow any other way. She only survives as we remember her life, mark her birthdays, etc."

It is not wise to rush in with idle chatter, but neither is it helpful to avoid the subject because it is unpleasant. Talking enables people to work their way through grief, and talk is a two-way street. Happy is the person who has the ear and the heart of a trusted and sensitive friend with whom to make the journey.

Be human. Show your humanity. Express your love. Weep with those who weep. Discover the value of physical contact. Anthony M. Kuchan, chairman of the psychology department at Marquette University, said, "We have all kinds of evidence that touching is absolutely essential to the development of human beings."

A young lady whose marriage had foundered told her mother that the thing she missed most was not having someone hold her in his arms.

"Don't try to prove anything to a survivor," Joseph Bayly wrote. "An arm about the shoulder, a firm grip of the hand, a kiss; these are the proofs that grief needs, not logical reasoning."[14]

Be cordial. Attend the funeral, send flowers, sign the guest book, write a note, make a call. I kept every card and letter sent to me when my brother died. The pastor of one of the largest churches on the West Coast canceled a long-standing speaking engagement to attend Dad's funeral. Our family will never forget that. You will never know until it happens what it means to have someone say, "We've been praying for you."

Be hospitable. Open your heart and home to the hurting. Include them in dinner parties and social gatherings. *Do not assume the widow is doing fine because she does not dress in mourning.* Remember that grief is a process and that the grieving desperately need friends and family to walk with them until healing comes.

"We lost a lot of friends when my dad died," a teenager told me. What did she mean? When her father died, her mother was suddenly a widow — and singles don't fit in the world of couples.

We will not understand grief or begin to support the grieving until we are willing to overlook our own comfort and extend ourselves as the Scriptures teach: "Pure and undefiled religion before God and the Father is this: to visit orphans and widows in their trouble" (James 1:27).

Be spiritually sensitive. The claims of Christ can be presented when the heart is tender. Paul Tournier wrote, "I fail to see how anyone who does not believe in the on-going life in Christ can live through the grief which follows death or the knowledge of a loved one's incurable illness. I have never understood that."[15]

The first thought that swept over me as I stood at my father's casket was: "There's no sting here." There was a sense of loss — but no bitterness or regret. The sting of death was absent and the room was filled with the peace of God. Only Christ can do that.

No wonder Tournier could say, "The human heart does not obey the rules of logic; it is constitutionally contradictory. I can truly say that I have a great grief and that I am a happy man."[16]

Endnotes
1. "Grief Recovery — 2," by Larry Yeagley, *Ministry International Journal for Pastors*, http://www.ministrymagazine.org/archive/1983/November/grief-recovery%E2%80%942.
2. Donald Grey Barnhouse, *Eternity* magazine.

3. C.S. Lewis, *A Grief Observed* (San Francisco, CA: Harper, 1989).
4. Paul Tournier, *Eternity* magazine.
5. Doug Manning, *Don't Take My Grief Away* (San Francisco, CA: Harper, 1984).
6. Paul E. Meier and Frank B. Minirth, *Happiness Is a Choice* (Grand Rapids, MI: Baker Book House, 1981).
7. John Kennedy and Lee Oser, *The Everything Guide to C.S. Lewis & Narnia* (Avon, MA: Adams Media, 2008), p. 248.
8. http://www.goodreads.com/author/quotes/4196101.Kahlil_Gibran.
9. "Tell It to Jesus," words by Edmund S. Lorenz, 1876.
10. William H. Frey and Muriel Langseth, *Crying: The Mystery of Tears* (Minneapolis, MN: Winston Press, 1985), p. 26.
11. http://www.ministrymagazine.org/archive/1987/September/when-tragedy-strikes-the-pastor.
12. Joseph Bayly, *Eternity* magazine.
13. Manning, *Don't Take My Grief Away.*
14. Joe Bayly, *View from a Hearse* (Elgin, IL: D.C. Cook Pub. Co., 1973).
15. Paul Tournier, *Eternity* magazine.
16. Ibid.

How far away is heaven? It is not so far as some imagine. It wasn't very far from Daniel. It was not so far off that Elijah's prayer and those of others could not be heard there. Men full of the Spirit can look right into heaven.

(Dwight Lyman Moody, 1837–1899)

CHAPTER SIX
THE TRUTH
ABOUT HEAVEN

Whatever became of heaven? The last century saw a flood of books published on the subject of the life beyond, but only a few really significant volumes have appeared in the last 50 years. Yet, as Ian Maclaren declared, "One must be affected with spiritual stupidity or cursed with incurable frivolity who has never thought of that new state on which he may enter at any time."[1]

A hundred years ago, T. DeWitt Talmage had one of the largest congregations of any preacher in the world. Once when visiting a friend who was dying, Talmage bade him farewell and said, "Give my love to my boy," referring to his son, DeWitt, who had died years before.

C.S. Lewis wrote that "a continual look-ing forward to the eternal world is not as some modern people think a form of escapism or wishful thinking, but one of the things a Christian is meant to do."[2] Heaven has always been the home of the soul and the hope of the believer. The old hymn said, "I will meet you in the morning, just inside the Eastern Gate" and was a promise we intended to keep. When days grew long and nights seemed never to end, we dreamed of a place where there is no night, of a land where we'll never grow old.

Bishop Hughes, a godly Methodist of a generation ago, told a group of his preach-ers, "Brethren, I am on my way to heaven and I don't intend to get lost."

Well, the poor bishop would be quite out of place in our world. We are far too sophis-ticated for that kind of thing. The unbelief of modern man is described by the poet Emily Dickinson:

> Those — dying then
> Knew where they went —
> They went to God's right hand.
> That hand is amputated now
> And God cannot be found.

This generation scorns the simple faith of a man who embraces divine revelation. Harvard philosopher Alfred North Whitehead once asked a friend, "As for Christian theology, can you imagine anything more appallingly idiotic than the Christian idea of heaven?"[3]

Canon B.H. Streeter, a New Testament scholar considered somewhat orthodox, in a famous essay, wrote, "The heaven of Sunday school teaching or popular hymnology is a place which the plain man does not believe to exist, and which he would not want to go to when he died."[4]

Is it not strange in a world like ours, poised as it is on the brink of judgment, that so little thought is given to our eternal destiny? Philip Yancey wrote, "I have watched in hospital groups as dying patients worked desperately toward a calm stage of acceptance. Strangely, no one ever talked about heaven in those groups; it seemed embarrassing, somehow cowardly. What convulsion of values can have us holding up the prospect of annihilation as brave and that of blissful eternity as cowardly?"[5]

Even in the Church we are occupied with present blessings of a dozen varieties and have long since ceased to celebrate heaven in sermon and song. And what have we gained by discounting the future life?

"If you read history," C.S. Lewis observed, "you will find that Christians who did most for the present world were just those who thought most of the next. It is since Christians have largely ceased to think of the other world that they have become so ineffective in this."[6]

Either there is a heaven or there is not. "If there is not," Lewis argues, "then Christianity is false, for this doctrine is woven into its whole fabric." If that is the case, if there is a land that is fairer than day, if it is true that "earth has no sorrow that heaven cannot heal,"[7] let us pursue the wondrous vision. "If then you were raised with Christ, seek those things which are above, where Christ is, sitting at the right hand of God. Set your mind on things above, not on things on the earth" (Col. 3:1–2).

Rabbi Harold Kushner wrote, "Neither I nor any other living person can know anything about the reality of that hope."[8] Is he right? Does any living person know what, if anything, awaits a man when he dies? Is there a place where wrongs are made right and where tears are dried? Is human life but a picture drawn on a canvas to be erased and forgotten? What is this longing in my soul for a land I have never seen? What is this sense of loneliness which suddenly descends upon my soul, this hunger for something I cannot name and do not know? What is the real truth about heaven?

Heaven is a place. That is to say that heaven is real. It is not a figment of imagination. It is not vague; it is specific. Jesus said, "Let not your heart be troubled; you believe in God, believe also in Me. In My Father's house are many mansions; if it were not so, I would have told you. I go to prepare a place for you. And if I go and prepare a place for you, I will come again and receive you to Myself; that where I am, there you may be also" (John 14:1–4).

After the death of Donald Grey Barnhouse, his wife drove home from the hospital. Grandchildren heard her coming and came crashing down the stairs, wildly exclaiming, "Grandma! Have you heard the news? Granddaddy's in heaven!

"Grandma, he's talking to Abraham — and David — and Lazarus — and Martha and Mary — and Peter and John and Andrew.

"Grandma, *he* can SEE *Jesus!*"[9]

Your loved ones who died in Christ are with the Lord! Think of it! Can you imagine what it's like? Think of the people they have seen: patriarchs and prophets, apostles and martyrs, loved ones and old friends. Let your imagination run wild. Little wonder the Apostle Paul said, "For I am hard pressed between the two, having a desire to depart and be with Christ, which is far better (Phil. 1:23).

Paul Tournier wrote, "Since my wife's death I have come to realize that I had lived all my life in mourning, waiting for reunion with my parents. Nelly had felt that this was so, because just before she died she said to me she would meet them there. So I have lived my whole life in their unseen presence, in the atmosphere of faith, love, and poetry that characterized their own lives. Now, with my new bereavement, my link with heaven is made stronger still."[10]

My brother David was deeply involved in the planning and construction of new facilities for his church. He offered to provide all the landscaping and painting. A night or two after planting a row of red leaf maple trees along the road, someone stole them. After David's death, our brother Clayton's gifted pen gave us these words: "I had a fanciful idea that old Davey — due to the abruptness and all of his last trip — was relieved and terribly pleased to see, first thing upon arrival, the great forest-stand of red leaf maples that formed the first boulevard he happened to see. . . . I tried once to relieve his disappointment, and anger even, over the loss of a few red leaf maples along the church's front boulevard by saying, 'Well, David, if you gave them to Him — don't worry, He's got them. They're just transplanted, you see.' "

Heaven is a real place.

But what shall we do there? What are the activities of heaven? I think all would agree with Bible teacher and author

Wilbur M. Smith that "the first great and continuous activity for the redeemed will be *worship* of the triune God." He suggests that many of the Psalms will have their perfect fulfillment in those days of eternal bliss[11] (see Ps. 29:2, 95:6, 96:9, 132:7; Heb. 1:6).

It is interesting to note that the last book in the Bible is filled with songs. There are 13 in all, sung by elders, angels, and the redeemed. What glory awaits us when we enter the visible presence of the Lord!

Heaven is a place of *service.* "And there shall be no more curse, but the throne of God and of the Lamb shall be in it, and His servants shall serve Him" (Rev. 22:3). David Gregg wrote in *Heaven Life*:

> It is work as free from care and toil and fatigue as is the wingstroke of the jubilant lark when it soars into the sunlight of a fresh, clear day and, spontaneously and for self-relief, pours out its thrilling carol. Work up there is a matter of self-relief, as well as a matter of obedience to the

ruling will of God. It is work according to one's tastes and delight and ability. If tastes vary there, if abilities vary there, then occupations will vary there.[12]

And think of the *fellowship* we shall enjoy. The anticipation of seeing our Lord Jesus Christ, the saints of all ages, as well as our own dear ones who await us is one of the deepest joys of the Christian life. *And, of course, we shall know our loved ones in heaven.* Paul's words, intended to bring comfort to the Thessalonians, would be meaningless were it not so: "Comfort one another with these words" (1 Thess. 4:18).

Death will not permanently separate loved ones who died in Christ. We will meet again and know each other.

When King David's baby boy died, he said, "I shall go to him, but he shall not return to me" (2 Sam. 12:23). He intended to meet his child in heaven and know that child. Moses and Elijah appeared with Jesus on the Mount of Transfiguration and the disciples knew them, and in heaven we shall instantly know each other, the limitations and frailties of human life gone forever.

"I still feel that the dearest here will be dearer there in a way I could never know in this world," wrote the Methodist evangelist Vance Havner. "My Father knows how to do it and seconds after I arrive, all my questions will have disappeared in ecstasy as I take up my abode in the house of the Lord forever."[13]

I am taking the liberty to quote a lengthy paragraph from *Future State* by Archbishop Richard Whately. It beautifully describes the cultivation of friendships we shall enjoy in our heaven:

> I am convinced that the extension and perfection of friendship will constitute a great part of the future happiness of the blest. Many have lived in various and distant ages and countries, who have been in their characters — I mean not merely in their being generally *estimable*, but — in the agreement of their tastes, and suitableness of

disposition, perfectly adapted for friendship with each other, but who of course could never *meet* in this world. Many a one selects, when he is reading history — a truly pious Christian most especially in reading sacred history — some one or two favorite characters with whom he feels that a personal acquaintance would have been peculiarly delightful to him. Why should not such a desire be realized in a future state? A wish to see and personally know, for example, the Apostle Paul, or John, is the most likely to arise in the noblest and purest mind. I should be sorry to think such a wish absurd and presumptuous, or unlikely ever to be gratified. The highest enjoyment doubtless to the blest will be the personal knowledge of their great and beloved Master. Yet I cannot but think that some part of their happiness will consist in an intimate knowledge of the greatest of His followers also; and of those of them in particular whose peculiar qualities are, to each, the most peculiarly attractive. In this world, again, our friendships are limited not only to those who live in the same age and country, but to a small portion even of those who are not unknown to us, and whom we know to be estimable and amiable, and whom, we feel, *might* have been among our dearest friends. Our command of *time and leisure* to cultivate friendships imposes a limit to their extent; they are bounded rather by the occupation of our *thoughts,* than of our *affections.*[14]

There is great practical value in believing what the Scriptures teach about the life to come. John Wesley, in a letter to John Smith dated June 25, 1746, wrote: "I desire to have both heaven and hell ever in my eye while I stand in this isthmus of life between these two boundless oceans; and I verily think the daily consideration of both highly becomes all men of reason and religion."[15]

Warren Wiersbe observed that "to Jesus Christ, heaven was not simply a destination; it was a motivation. As He faced the cross, He said, 'The hour is come for the Son of Man to be glorified' " (John 12:23).[16]

That glorious hope is expressed in one of the many hymns written by Fanny Crosby, who lived most of her life in total blindness:

> When my life work is ended,
> and I cross the swelling tide,
> When the bright and glorious morning
> I shall see;
> I shall know my Redeemer
> when I reach the other side,
> And His smile will be
> the first to welcome me.[17]

When a visitor enters Westminster Abbey in London, he is given a folder which describes the famous place where worship has been offered continuously for nearly 900 years. Included is this sentence: "WE ASK YOU — as you walk around to remember that you are on holy ground — to behave with reverence — to speak quietly — and do not forget to look up very often if you wish to see the glory of this Church."

I like that line: *Do not forget to look up.* . . . Remember that when you're drying dishes or drying tears, when you're lonely or afraid. Someone said, "The years slip by like grace notes in a song; it's the days and the nights that get long."

When they do — *look up!*

> The strife will not be long;
> This day the noise of battle,
> The next, the victor's song.[18]

Dear friend, I will meet you — in the morning — just inside the Eastern Gate — over there.

Endnotes
1. Wilbur M. Smith, *Biblical Doctrine of Heaven* (Chicago, IL: Moody Press, 1968).
2. C.S. Lewis, *A Grief Observed* (San Francisco, CA: Harper, 1989).
3. Warren W. Wiersbe, *The Bible Exposition Commentary* (Colorado Springs, CO: David C. Cook, 2004), p. 120.
4. Smith, *Biblical Doctrine of Heaven.*
5. Philip Yancey, "Heaven Can't Wait," *Christianity Today*, 6/1/2003, http://www.christianitytoday.com.
6. Lewis, *A Grief Observed.*
7. Thomas Moore, "Come Ye Disconsolate,"1886.

8. Harold S. Kushner, *When Bad Things Happen to Good People* (New York: Avon Books, 1981), p. 28.

9. Margaret Barnhouse, *That Man Barnhouse* (Wheaton, IL: Tyndale House, 1983).

10. Paul Tournier, *Eternity* magazine.

11. Smith, *Biblical Doctrine of Heaven.*

12. Ibid.

13. Havner, *Though I Walk Through the Valley* (Old Tappan, NJ: F.H. Revell, 1974).

14. Smith, *Biblical Doctrine of Heaven.*

15. Ibid.

16. Wiersbe, *Why Us? When Bad Things Happen to God's People.*

17. Fanny Crosby, "My Savior First of All," 1891.

18. George Duffield, "Stand Up, Stand Up for Jesus," 1858.

I laugh and shout for life

is good, though my feet

are set in silent ways.

(Helen Adams Keller, 1880–1968)

CHAPTER SEVEN
GETTING ON
WITH LIFE

Life is to be lived, not avoided. Hope deferred makes the heart sick. The time comes when you must pick up the pieces of a broken heart and get on with life. "He is already half false who speculates on truth and does not do it," F.W. Robertson wrote. "Truth is given, not to be contemplated but to be done. Life is an action—not a thought."[1]

A friend of mine says that the difference between what you are and what you want to be is what you do.

Let me suggest 10 positive steps you can take — things you can do — to rebuild a broken life, to rediscover the joy of living.

STEP 1 — *Deal with grief.* "It is hard to have patience with people who say, 'There is no death,' or 'Death doesn't matter,'" C.S. Lewis writes with some impatience after the death of his wife. "There *is* death. And whatever *is* matters. And whatever happens has consequences, and it and they are irrevocable and irreversible. You might as well say that birth doesn't matter. . . . She died. She is dead. Is the word so difficult?"[2]

John Milton, the blind poet, wrote, "It is not miserable to be blind; it is miserable to be incapable of enduring blindness."[3]

Face up to the loss. Don't linger in the world of fantasy. Accept what you cannot change. Be honest about the pain you feel.

STEP 2 — *Maintain a positive and hopeful attitude.* In one of his first letters after going away to college, my son wrote simply, "Life is tough; I am tougher." He was learning the profound truth expressed by Dr. Sam Shoemaker, a founder of Alcoholics Anonymous, churchman, soul winner, and preacher: "There are, in every situation, two factors: there is what happens, and there is how we take what happens."[4]

Victor Frankl wrote, "Everything can be taken from a man but one thing — the last of the human freedoms — to choose one's attitude in any given circumstance.''[5]

Dale E. Galloway tells this story in *Dream a New Dream*: An eminent German Jewish doctor was arrested by the Gestapo during World War II. As he was being interrogated by the Nazi secret police, he was stripped of all his possessions — his clothes, his jewelry, his wedding band. He was imprisoned for days without knowing whether his family was alive or dead. His head was shaved. He was repeatedly taken from his prison cell and forced to stand naked under bright lights through grueling periods of questioning. He underwent many savage and senseless tortures. He later said that, stripped of everything, he realized he had only one thing left: 'I realized I still had the power to choose my own attitude. No matter what happened now, the attitude choice was mine to make. Bitterness or forgiveness, to give up or to go on, hatred or hope — the attitude was still mine and no one in the Gestapo could take away my attitude.' ''[6]

Life is tough — there's no question about it, but *you are tougher*! The Apostle

Paul wrote, "I can do all things through Christ who strengthens me" (Phil. 4:13).

STEP 3 — *Retain your sense of humor.* Foolish remarks are never more out of place than at a funeral, but honest humor is sanctifying. It can also be a great relief, as it was at my dad's memorial service. The pastor, something of a perfectionist, said, "How many times I went to the pulpit, my sermon ready, and the order of service carefully laid out. Then Pastor Johnson prayed for 15 minutes and blew the whole schedule."

We chuckled as we chased the tears that bounced off our noses.

The Bible says, "A merry heart does good, like medicine, but a broken spirit dries the bones" (Prov. 17:22).

Humor enables you to see through things — to reach past the chaos and pain of the present and find the bottom line. Someone said that humor is the lotion for the sunburns of life. A happy spirit, even when there are tears, will go a long way toward healing skinned knees and bruised elbows, shattered bones and sprained ankles, as well as mending broken hearts and broken dreams.

STEP 4 — *Look at your loss from the other's point of view.* When Ron Redlich died a few days before Christmas, our church secretary mused, "Just think, Ron's home for the holidays."

That's it! I thought. *That's it!* We have been looking at this from our point of view. We are sad like you are sad when a loved one flies away after a visit. But even as your eyes watch the departing plane become smaller and smaller, other eyes are searching the sky as the same plane becomes larger and larger. Tears of sorrow here are shouts of joy there.

And so it is, departed loved ones who have died in Christ are in the Father's house, safe forever, never again to weep or suffer pain. I often think of them when I go to church: *They're there! They have seen Jesus* — and I rejoice.

STEP 5 — *Help somebody. Avoid isolation.* Get involved with others. Do not bury your hurt inside. Convert your loss into an opportunity for compassion and involvement.

Someone said, "The mind grows by taking in, but the heart grows by giving out." Is there anywhere a better example of "giving out" than the proud firefighters of New York after 9/11? "I will never look at a firefighter the same way again," said the Rev. Bill Hybels of Willow Creek Community Church. "What is it in someone, hundreds of them, to compel them to run into a burning building, while everyone is running out, just to save people they don't even know? Their bravery has become part of our national legacy."[7]

Parents who lost a child wrote, "Many of you have asked what you can do to help us. We are asking, pleading, please give your kids an extra hug and kiss, an extra word of praise and love, a few extra moments of your time during the busy days we all have."

A few days after my father died, Mother received a letter from a woman who attended my brother's church in South Carolina. "I only had one baby," she wrote, "and he was stillborn. All the time I carried him I dreamed of the day I would stand at the altar and dedicate that baby to God. Since I didn't get to realize that dream, I have just loved other babies, and that is what led me to volunteer my secretarial skills at a home for unwed mothers. Every once in a while I get to keep one of the babies for three or four days for a foster parent. Only God knows the joy that floods my soul when I am privileged to love, hug, kiss, and rock a newborn baby."

Paul wrote, "Blessed be the God and Father of our Lord Jesus Christ, the Father of mercies and God of all comfort, who comforts us in all our tribulation, that we may be able to comfort those who are in any trouble, with the comfort with which we ourselves are comforted by God. For as the sufferings of Christ abound in us, so our consolation also abounds through Christ" (2 Cor. 1:3–5).

STEP 6 — *Get the big picture.* Too often we view life from our own limited perspective. Little men, born yesterday and dying tomorrow, with eyes that can't see a day ahead, are ill-prepared to measure the movements and meaning of a mind that is eternal.

Author Stephen Rexroat called late one evening and said, "Dan, let me tell you a story." It went something like this:

> Steve is driving across the
> Midwest and stops at a church to

thank the pastor for the support his
church has provided. The parking
lot is crowded, and upon entering
the church he discovers a meeting in progress. He would go on
his way, but the secretary urges
him to stay. "Go on in," she says,
"the pastor would like to see you."
Steve goes in and sits down in the
back. An elderly minister gets up to
speak. "Let me tell you about King
David," he begins. "David had a
dream. He will build a house for
God, a magnificent temple. People
will come from all over to see it
and to worship in it. So David hires
architects, gathers supplies and gets
the financing in place when the Lord
sends a prophet who tells David
he is not to proceed. After some
time, David dies. He leaves behind
drawings, blueprints, designs, and
his own treasure of gold and silver.
His son Solomon assumes the task
and builds the temple. A day is set
for dedication and the people come

and they worship. After many years the great building is destroyed, torn down. Only a wall remains. But you know," the minister continues, "the Twenty-third Psalm, which David wrote, is still with us."

"Think of it," Steve says, "the Twenty-third Psalm has only 118 words in it, but it has outlived the centuries and been quoted a million times and continues to comfort the people of God."

That's the big picture. The Scriptures teach that those things which are seen are temporal, but those things which are not seen are eternal. Buildings are erected and demolished. Cities come and go. Kings rise and fall. The fashion of this world passes away, but, as the dying John Wesley cried, "The best of all is, God is with us."[8]

STEP 7 — *Deepen your relationship with God.* Find strength in prayer. During World War II, an unknown soldier in a trench in Tunisia left behind a note with the verse:

Stay with me God
The night is dark,
The night is cold,
My little spark
Of courage dies.
The night is long,
Be with me God
And make me strong.

Communion with God was a source of comfort and strength for Paul Tournier after the death of his wife, as evidenced by these words: "Nowadays, for example, to pray is to turn home," he wrote. "For then they run to meet us, draw us with their dear familiar hands into the Presence, stand closer to us the whole time we are there — quite close while we are there."[9]

Employ your sorrows; make them work for you. Let disappointment drive you deep into the heart of God.

I have always loved *The Marshes of Glynn* by Sidney Lanier. After spending a day in the woods and beside the salt marshes of Glynn County, Georgia, the poet writes these wonderful lines:

> As the marsh-hen secretly builds
> on the watery sod,
> Behold, I will build me a nest
> on the greatness of God.

The marshes are flooded when the tide comes in, yet the marsh-hen, instead of flying away, builds her nest in the tough roots of the grasses. Observing the courage of the marsh-hen in the face of storm and flood, the poet's troubles seemed to drop away. One cannot escape the storm, but one can "fly in the greatness of God as the marsh-hen flies." Let's say it together:

> I will heartily lay me a hold
> on the greatness of God —

STEP 8 — *Trust God to turn tragedy into triumph.* After the death of author Joseph Bayly, Dr. C. Everett Koop said, "To me, Joe's finest moment was when he rose before a standing-room-only crowd at his oldest son's memorial service, and with contracted throat and overwhelming grief, said, 'I've come to talk with you about my earthly son and our Heavenly Father.' Numerous college students in the audience met Christ that night."[10]

The enemies of freedom accomplished more than they intended when they converted airplanes into bombs and set the tip of Manhattan on fire. The attack struck a dormant chord within our people. It was like pouring gas on smoldering embers. The back of cynicism was broken. A slumbering patriotism sprang forth. One hundred and sixteen thousand American flags were sold by Wal-Mart before the sun went down that day.

Do you ever wonder what happened to those shrill voices that have clamored for the dismissal of God in public life? For a great while now, the good Lord has been treated like a pariah in our midst. He may send the rain on the just and on the unjust and freely give us the next breath we draw, but we have been uneasy with God around. For now, at least, the whiners have fallen strangely silent.

"God is back," columnist Peggy Noonan wrote.[11] With the president exhorting us to pray, and praying himself, with congressional leaders praying in the Capitol, with people flocking to churches and synagogues and singing "God Bless America" at sporting events — with all our imperfections and notwithstanding our need of repentance, we are still one nation under God.

When the enemy intends evil, remember, God is not dead nor does He sleep, and He is quite able to transform tragedy into triumph.

STEP 9 — *Get on with life.* Jesus said, "I have come that they may have life" (John 10:10). We must live, and live fully. Jim Elliot, the young missionary martyr, wrote, "Wherever you are, be all there. Live to the hilt every situation you believe to be the will of God."[12]

"Life cannot wait until the sciences may have explained the universe scientifically," wrote Jose Ortego of Gasset. "We cannot put off living until we are ready. Life is fired at us point blank."[13]

The principle applies to individuals, to churches, to a country. What does a great nation do when assaulted? How does it respond to unprovoked attack? Is it a time to retreat, to run for cover? Or shall we assess the damage, chart a new course, and get moving? Remember what Jesus said when He healed the lame man: "Take up your bed and walk" (John 5:8).

A hundred times I have paused to ponder the words on a plaque which hangs on a wall in our home:

> Mend a quarrel. Search out a forgotten friend. Dismiss suspicion, and replace it with trust. Write a love letter. Share some treasure. Give a soft answer. Encourage youth. Manifest your loyalty in a word or deed. Keep a promise. Find the time. Forego a grudge. Forgive an enemy. Listen. Apologize if you were wrong. Try to understand. Flout envy. Examine your demands on others. Think first of someone else. Appreciate, be kind, be gentle. Laugh a little more. Deserve confidence. Take up arms against malice. Decry complacency. Express your gratitude. Worship your God. Gladden the heart of a

child. Take pleasure in the beauty and wonder of the earth. Speak your love. Speak it again. Speak it still again. Speak it still once again.

A great general said that the secret of success in battle is in getting good and ready. Now that you are good and ready, take the first step.

STEP 10 — *Stand up in praise to God.* There is an exquisite paragraph in a famous sermon by Arthur John Gossip:

> Do you think Christ always understood or found it easy? There was a day when He took God's will for Him into His hand, and turned it round, and looked at it. And, "Is this what You ask of Me?" He said; and for a moment His eyes looked almost incredulous. Aye, and another day when, puzzled and uncertain, He cried out, "But is this really what You mean that I should give You, this here and now?" Yes, and another still, when the cold rushing waters roared in a raging torrent

through His soul yet He would not turn back, and fought His way to the farther bank, died still believing in the God who seemed to have deserted Him. And that is why He is given a name that is above every name.[14]

There comes a moment when we forget our pain and are transfixed by a vision of His loveliness; He who, in the words of David Hubbard, "looted death of its strangeness and plundered it of its judgment."[15]

Charles Spurgeon said, "God is too good to be unkind, too wise to be mistaken; and when you cannot trace His hand, you can always trust His heart."[16]

The parents of Ronald Redlich, referred to earlier, long ago learned to trust His heart when they could not trace His hand, and their unwillingness to surrender to bitterness, cynicism or despair was graphically demonstrated by an incident at Ron's funeral.

As the pastor rose to conclude the service, my eyes surveyed the audience and shifted to the area reserved for the family. "Let us close this service," the pastor said, "by singing 'How Great Thou Art.' The family may remain seated, but let the rest of us stand and sing together."

Then occurred one of those things you never forget. Leonard Redlich, the grieving father, rose to his feet. He stood erect like an unbowed oak. Then his wife rose and stood beside her husband. Now everyone was standing, and a great anthem of praise ascended to heaven.

"The family may remain seated," the pastor had said, but the family rose as if to say, "Our hearts may be bowed in grief, our eyes blinded by tears, but when the people rise to worship the Lord, we too shall stand! We shall not be spectators when it's time to stand up in praise to God!"

The family may remain seated! Shall the birds cease their singing or the sun refuse to shine? Remain seated! Can it be? Shall the heavens declare the glory of God and the earth show His handiwork — and our lips be silent? Must these stones cry out in praise to God?

Let the sound of our praise resound from the jungle to the desert, and from the city to the country. Let it ricochet from mountain peak to mountain peak and cascade down a thousand mountain streams. Let it tumble across the prairie, whisper through the wind, shout in the storm and sing in the night. Let everything that has breath praise the Lord!

Endnotes
1. Warren Wiersbe, *Why Us? When Bad Things Happen to God's People* (Grand Rapids, MI: Baker Book House, 1984).
2. C.S. Lewis, *A Grief Observed* (San Francisco, CA: Harper, 1989).
3. http://www.answers.com/topic/john-milton.
4. Helen Smith Shoemaker, *I Stand by the Door* (Irving, TX: Word, Inc., 1978).
5. Victor Frankl, *Dream a New Dream* (Sisters, OR: Multnomah Books).
6. Ibid.
7. *Newsweek* (December 3, 2001).
8. wesley.nnu.edu/john...the.../chapter-xix-the-passing-of-john-wesley.
9. Paul Tournier, *Eternity* magazine.
10. *Eternity* magazine.
11. Peggy Noonan, "God Is Back," listserv.virtueonline.org/pipermail/virtueonline...org/.../002796.html.
12. www.goodreads.com/author/quotes/2125255.Jim_Elliot.
13. Wiersbe, *Why Us? When Bad Things Happen to God's People.*

14. Arthur John Gossip, "When Life Tumbles in, What Then," 1927, http://www.brianiscool.com/arthur-john-gossip.html.
15. David Hubbard, *Why Do I Have to Die?* (Ventura, CA: Gospel Light Publications.
16. www.baptistcourier.com/4948.article.

"INK
ON PAPER
TO TOUCH
ETERNITY"

join us

New Leaf Press
A Division of New Leaf Publishing Group

When your life is in God's hands,
every day is your best day.

DEVOTIONAL THOUGHTS *by* ROY LESSIN

Today
is Your Best Day

DISCOVERING
GOD'S BEST
for YOU

$14.99 | 978-0-89221-710-6 | Casebound

nlpg.com/**yourbestday**